€12.94.   J709

Emotion & Relationships

Jane Bingham

www.raintreepublishers.co.uk

Visit our website to find out more information about **Raintree** books.

To order:
☎ Phone 44 (0) 1865 888113
📄 Send a fax to 44 (0) 1865 314091
💻 Visit the Raintree bookshop at **www.raintreepublishers.co.uk** to browse our catalogue and order online.

First published in Great Britain by Raintree,
Halley Court, Jordan Hill, Oxford OX2 8EJ,
part of Harcourt Education.

Raintree is a registered trademark of Harcourt Education Ltd.

© Harcourt Education Ltd 2006
First Published in paperback in 2007
The moral right of the proprietor has been asserted.

Editorial: Isabel Thomas and Rosie Gordon
Design: Richard Parker & Tinstar Design www.tinstar.com
Picture Research: Hannah Taylor and Zoe Spilberg
Production: Duncan Gilbert

Originated by Chroma Graphics
Printed and bound in Hongkong

10 digit ISBN 1 4062 0151 0 (hardback)
13 digit ISBN 978 1 4062 0151 2

10 09 08 07 06
10 9 8 7 6 5 4 3 2 1

10 digit ISBN 1 4062 0158 8 (paperback)
13 digit ISBN 978 1 4062 0158 1

10 09 08 07
10 9 8 7 6 5 4 3 2 1

British Library Cataloguing in Publication Data
Bingham, Jane
    Emotion and relationships. - (Through artists' eyes)
I.Title
    704.9'491524

Acknowledgements
The publishers would like to thank the following for permission to reproduce photographs: © 2006 Banco de México Diego Rivera & Frida Kahlo Museums Trust. Av. Cinco de Mayo No. 2, Col. Centro, Del. Cuauhtémoc 06059, México, D.F.: **p. 33**, Photo: Bridgeman Art Library/ Palacio Nacional, Mexico City, Mexico, Sean Sprague/ Mexicolore; **p. 41**, © 2000, Photo Schalkwijk/ Scala, Florence. **P. 43**, © 2000, Photo Smithsonian American Art Museum/ Art Resource/ Scala, Florence; **p. 22**, © ADAGP, Paris and DACS, London 2006 Photo: © 2005. Digital Image, The Museum of Modern Art, New York/ Scala, Florence. Acquired through the Lillie P.Bliss Bequest; **p. 23**, © ADAGP, Paris and DACS, London 2006 Photo: Bridgeman Art Library/ Private Collection, © Christie's Images; **p. 42**, © ADAGP, Paris and DACS, London, 2006 Photo: Museum Moderner Kunst; **p. 51**, © ARS, NY and DACS, London 2006 Photo: © 2005, Digital Image, The Museum of Modern Art, New York/ Scala, Florence. The Sidney and Harriet Janis Collection; **p. 49**, © DACS 2006 Photo: 1990, Photo Scala, Florence- courtesy of the Ministero Beni e Att. Culturali; **p. 5**, © Munch Museum/ Munch- Ellingsen Group, BONO, Oslo, DACS, London 2006 Photo: 1990, Photo Scala, Florence/ Nasjonalgalleriet; **p. 45**, © Succession Picasso/ DACS 2006 Photo: Bridgeman Art Library/ © The Barnes Foundation, Merion, Pennsylvania, USA; **p. 31**, © Trustess of the National Museums of Scotland; Bridgeman Art Library **pp. 11** (The work illustrated on page 11 has been reproduced by permission of the Henry Moore Foundation; **38**, (© Ashmolean Museum, University of Oxford, UK), **39**, (© Birmingham Museums and Art Gallery; **p. 10**, (Bridgeman Art Library) © Butler Institute of American Art, Youngstown, OH, USA, Museum Purchase 1947), **20, 25** (© Wallace Collection, London, UK), **9**, (© Yale Centre for British Art, Paul Mellon Collection, USA), **37**, (Basilique Saint-Denis, France, Lauros/ Giraudon), **46**, (Goethe Museum, Frankfurt, Germany, Peter Willi), **13**, (Musee d'Orsay, Paris, France, Giraudon), **16**, (Museo Archeologico Nazionale, Naples, Italy), **18**, (National Gallery, London, UK), **6**, (National Museum, Lagos, Nigeria, © Held Collection), **33**, (Palacio Nacional, Mexico City, Mexico, Sean Sprague/ Mexicolore), **44**, (Private Collection), **24**, (Private Collection. Giraudon), **19**, (Rijksmuseum, Amsterdam, Holland), **47**, (Victoria & Albert Museum, London, UK); **p. 7** Corbis Royalty Free; Corbis/ **pp. 34** (ART on FILE), **27, 30** (Asian Art & Archaeology, Inc.), **35**, (Danny Lehman), **15**, (David Turnley). **28**, (Historical Picture Archive), **26**, (Keren Su), **29**, Danny Lehman (Philip James Corwin), **21**, (Robbie Jack); **p.17**, The Art Archive / British Library; **p. 14**, www.tropix. xo.uk (Pam Howarth). **Cover**: *People in the Sun* 1960, Hopper, Edward (1882-1967). © 2000. Photo Smithsonian American Art Museum/ Art Resource/ Scala, Florence.

The publishers would like to thank Karen Hosack for her assistance in the preparation of this book.

Contents

Introduction 4

Family feelings 6

Love and marriage 14

Happiness and contentment 24

Anger, violence, and hatred 28

Grief, loss, and mourning 34

Sickness and pain 40

Fear, loneliness, and isolation 42

Dreams, nightmares, and fantasies 46

Art without emotion? 50

Map and Further reading 52

Timeline 53

Glossary 54

Index 56

Any words that appear in bold, **like this**, are explained in the glossary.

Introduction

A stranger is walking over a bridge towards you – you think it's a man but you can't be sure. All you know for certain is that whoever it is must be very upset. The mouth is wide open in a long, soundless scream. The hands are raised protectively to the skull-like face, and the eyes are staring wildly. Behind the screaming stranger are swirls of violent colour, and these disturbing shapes add to your feeling of panic. You feel sucked into the stranger's frightening world. But then you remind yourself – you are only looking at a painting.

When the Norwegian artist Edvard Munch first showed *The Scream* in 1893, many people hated it. Others thought it was a work of genius, but nobody could ignore it. Munch's work is so powerful because it expresses emotions that everybody recognizes. The question is: "Does the artist show his own deep feelings in *The Scream*, as well as connecting with ours?"

A range of feelings

For thousands of years, artists have created works of art that express feelings and emotions. These feelings can range from happiness and contentment to grief, anger, fear, and despair. Artists have also explored the disturbing sensations of sickness and pain, and the strange world of dreams and imagination. Some artists have tried to show how it feels to be in love. Others have explored different relationships, such as family love.

A range of art

This book covers art from the earliest times right up to the present day. It covers a range of different **media**, including painting, sculpture, and ceramics. It also mentions examples of poetry, stories, and films. Some of the works discussed here are by famous figures, such as Vincent Van Gogh, but many others are by lesser-known artists.

The art described in this book was made in countries all over the world. To help you to see exactly where a work of art was made, there is a world map on page 52. The timeline on page 53 provides an overview of the different periods of history discussed in the book.

Artists try to communicate through their work. The ideas their work shows can be conscious or unconscious. By looking carefully at these works of art, we can learn more about our own emotions and the feelings of others. Art can also make us think about the way we relate to other people.

Edvard Munch, *The Scream* (1893). This mysterious painting has a very disturbing effect on the viewer. Why is the person screaming, and who are the figures in the background? The dramatic, swirling colours help to create a sense of confusion and fear.

Family feelings

For thousands of years, artists have created images of their families. Today's family portraits usually show the artist's parents, partner, or children. However, in many societies, the idea of the family is much wider. Some families include all the members of a tribe. They can include the tribe's **ancestors**, stretching back to the distant past.

African ancestor figures

A tradition in some African societies is to carve figures of ancestors from wood. These carved figures are not meant to be a realistic likeness of a person. Instead, the carvings try to show what the person's spirit was like. To do this, certain features may be exaggerated or distorted.

This carving was made in the West African kingdom of Benin about 500 years ago. It shows the very powerful figure of a queen mother. The carving shows the queen's power and wealth, as she stares sternly straight ahead, wearing an elaborate headdress and collar.

Nobody is certain of the purpose of the mysterious Easter Island figures. But most experts agree that they represent powerful ancestor figures.

Carved ancestor figures are treated with great respect. They are often decorated with precious metals or other valuable materials. The wooden ancestor figures of the Bembe people, in the Congo, have eyes made from **porcelain**. This makes the figures look magical, as if they can see further than ordinary people.

Chinese ancestor portraits

In the 14th century CE, Chinese artists were painting **formal** "ancestor portraits". These full-length images were often painted on scrolls, which were passed down from one generation to the next. The portraits were hung in the family home. At special times during the year, the whole family gathered in front of the portrait and held a solemn ceremony to honour their ancestor.

Giant ancestors

The giant stone figures on Easter Island, in the South Pacific Ocean, were probably carved between 1400 and 1600 CE. **Archaeologists** believe that they represent powerful ancestor spirits. The giant figures all have their backs to the sea, perhaps to protect their people from harm.

Chinese ancestor paintings were accurate portraits. People believed that if their ancestor's portrait resembled somebody else, their family **rituals** could be directed to the wrong person. This could be very unlucky for their family.

Early portraits

The practice of painting family portraits didn't really take off until the 15th century. At this time, it became the fashion for rich Italian families to have their portraits painted.

Most early family portraits were very formal. They were painted mainly to show off a family's wealth. However, a few paintings provide a more **intimate** view of family life. Around 1460, Andrea Mantegna painted a series of **frescoes** featuring the wealthy Gonzaga family. The frescoes include a delightful scene showing the family welcoming their grown-up son home. In this **informal** painting, a young boy proudly holds his father's hand, and offers his other hand to his little brother.

Reynolds and Gainsborough

By the 18th century, it had become the custom for wealthy families to pose for their portraits. Two English artists, Sir Joshua Reynolds and Thomas Gainsborough, were both in great demand for family portraits. They painted parents with their children, all dressed up in their finery, gazing out at the artist. In these carefully arranged paintings, families pose at home amongst their prized possessions or against a tree in their **estate**. The portraits are clearly meant to show the family's wealth. However, some also manage to show close family feelings.

John Singleton Copley

The American artist John Singleton Copley was famous for his paintings of wealthy families, but one of his best-known portraits shows his own family. Copley had been apart from his family for several months when he painted *The Copley Family* in 1777, and the painting expresses his happiness that his family is united again. Copley's father-in-law and wife are both seated, while the artist stands behind them, working on a painting. At the centre of the painting are Copley's children. His oldest daughter stands staring solemnly outwards, looking grown-up and serious. Her smiling brother seems to be telling his mother a secret, while her younger sister leans comfortably on her mother's lap. Meanwhile, the baby is trying as hard as she can to attract her grandfather's attention.

Copley clearly knows his children very well, and each of them has their own personality. In the left-hand corner of the painting, Copley has painted an abandoned doll, adding to the impression of a relaxed family scene.

Thomas Gainsborough, *Mr and Mrs John Gravenor and their daughters, Elizabeth and Ann* (c.1754). This formal portrait is clearly intended to show off the family's wealth and land. However, Gainsborough has added some informal touches. The mother and the youngest girl have both taken off their sun hats, and the two daughters each hold a few wild flowers.

Mothers and children

Many artists have concentrated on the relationship of mothers and their children. The 17th-century Dutch painter Pieter de Hooch was one of the first European artists to **portray** scenes of everyday, family life. His paintings often feature mothers at home with their children. *A Woman Peeling Apples* shows a mother peeling a bowl of apples with her daughter by her side. The little girl holds an apple while her mother lifts up a long, twirling apple-skin to show it to her daughter. In this simple, happy scene, de Hooch has captured the close and loving relationship between the mother and her daughter.

Morisot and Cassatt

At the end of the 19th century, two artists were especially well known for painting images of mothers and children. The French painter Berthe Morisot and the American Mary Cassatt both painted in the **Impressionist** style. They used bold and confident brush strokes to create lively, colourful paintings.

One of Morisot's most famous paintings shows a mother gazing at her baby, who lies sleeping in a cradle. The young woman is beautiful and smartly dressed, but she is not aware of anything except her child. Morisot also painted scenes of women and older children. Her playful paintings *Hide-and-Seek* and *Butterfly Hunt* show mothers having fun with their young children.

Mary Cassatt was a painter and printmaker, who painted many pictures of women and children at home. One of her favourite subjects was a mother bathing her child. Cassatt also liked to show a mother sitting quietly with her child on her lap. Cassatt's pictures of mothers and children are filled with a sense of peacefulness and calm.

Mary Cassatt, *Agatha and her Child* (1891). Cassatt shows a real understanding of the special bond between mother and child.

Mother and child sculptures

The image of a mother and child appears in the sculpture of many different cultures. Many carvings from Africa show women holding babies. Often, these carvings show the simplified figure of a mother squatting on her heels and bending over her child. The mother's bent knees and long arms make a kind of cage to protect her baby.

Several modern **sculptors** have explored the theme of motherhood. In particular, the British sculptor Henry Moore has produced many **semi-abstract** works on the subject of the mother and child. Some of his sculptures are shaped like a mother lying on her side, cradling her baby inside the curves of her body. Others show an upright mother figure, hollowed out in the middle to enclose the shape of her child.

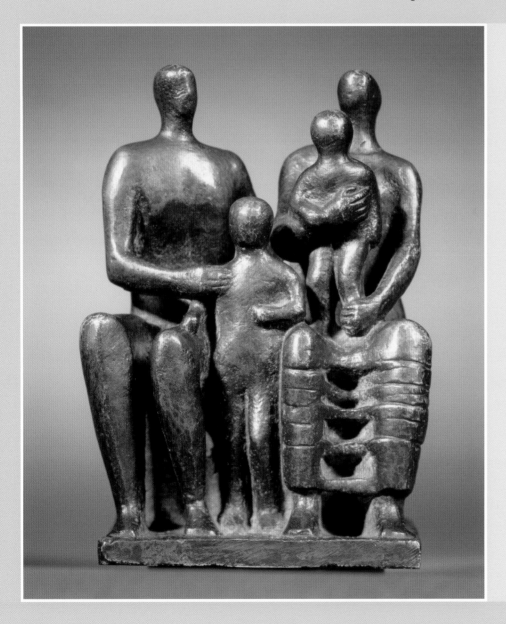

Henry Moore, *Family Group* (1901). Even though Moore's figures are greatly simplified, his sculpture still has a strong sense of family feeling. How do you think he has managed to show the relationship between the parents and their children?

Artists' children

Many artists have painted portraits of their own children. These images often show a special understanding of the children's personalities. The British painter Augustus John had many children, and he sometimes used them as subjects for his paintings. In John's striking portrait of his son Robin, the boy gazes straight out of the painting, as if he is looking into his father's eyes. His hair is untidy and he is frowning slightly as if he is tired of sitting still while his father paints him.

In 1618, the famous Dutch artist Peter Paul Rubens painted his daughter, Clara Serena. The little girl is half smiling at her father, and she looks intelligent and thoughtful. Rubens produced many drawings of his children, but the picture of Clara Serena appears to be his only painted portrait. Sadly, the little girl died when she was only twelve years old.

Artists' parents

Many famous artists have produced paintings of their parents. These very personal portraits are often full of tenderness for a much-loved person who is growing old.

In 1888, the Dutch painter Vincent van Gogh painted a portrait of his mother. Van Gogh sometimes painted pictures filled with torment (see page 44), but this is a cheerful, gentle image, painted in warm colours. It shows a strong-looking, smiling old woman, looking away slightly, as if she is remembering happy times.

In 1935, the Dutch artist M. C. Escher produced a fascinating portrait of his father. In many of his drawings, Escher liked to experiment with different ways of seeing things, but this is a realistic portrait. It shows an old gentleman looking with great interest at a paper through a magnifying glass. In this affectionate portrait, Escher gives us a clear idea of his father's character. Escher cleverly shows that, just like his son, his father is a man who is intensely interested in examining the world.

The American artist James McNeill Whistler produced a striking portrait of his mother. It was painted in 1871 and called *Arrangement in Grey and Black: Portrait of the Painter's Mother*. Whistler shows his mother sitting on a hard-backed chair, in a room that is almost bare. The old woman is solemn and unsmiling. She is dressed mainly in black and there is almost no colour in the painting.

At first sight, Whistler's portrait seems to be cold and lacking in emotion. But this is not true. Whistler deliberately showed his mother alone and dressed in black to illustrate her great strength of character.

She had just experienced tragedy – her husband and two of her children had died. Whistler shows her loneliness by placing her in an empty room, but there is a sign of hope and human connection. One of Whistler's paintings hangs on the wall behind his mother – a sign that she is not completely alone in the world.

James Abbot McNeill Whistler, *Arrangement in Grey and Black: Portrait of the Painter's Mother* (1871). In this striking portrait, the mother's face is the most colourful part of the painting. Why do you think Whistler chose to show so little colour in his portrait?

Love and marriage

All societies have rituals to celebrate **courtship** and marriage. In Western society, some women wear an engagement ring, and the bride and groom may wear special wedding clothes. These customs have a very long history. In other societies, many people still follow ancient customs. They produce works of art associated with courting and marriage.

African traditions

In some African tribal groups, young men and women perform courtship dances. These dances are a chance for young people to show off to each other before they choose a partner. Young Nuban men from East Africa prepare for their courtship dances by decorating their faces and bodies. They paint their faces with bold blocks of colour in white, black, red, and blue, and decorate their bodies with **abstract** patterns of swirls, triangles, and dots. This painting can take several hours to complete.

In parts of South Africa, girls send necklaces to the boys they love. Zulu girls make bead necklaces with coloured pendants hanging down from them. Each colour has a different meaning and together the colours make up a message. For example, red can stand for love, white for truth, and black for disappointment. Sometimes, Zulu young men wear several love messages at once.

Married women from the Ndebele tribe in southeast Africa wear a bridal "apron". This is a goatskin belt with decorated strips hanging down from it. The strips on a bride's belt represent the cattle that the bridegroom's family pays for his bride.

Some Zulu pendant necklaces, like the two this Zulu girl wears, have special significance as messages of love.

Indian brides

Indian brides wear beautiful **saris** and jewellery on their wedding day. Brides from the city of Varanasi, on the River Ganges, wear richly embroidered saris, and delicate jewellery made from gold and pearls. In the desert area of Rajastan, brides wear colourful saris decorated with mirrors. They also wear a lot of heavy silver jewellery.

The amount of jewellery that a Rajastani bride wears depends on how rich her husband is. If her husband is very wealthy, she may wear a pendant on her forehead, dangling earrings, a choker round her neck, a collection of bracelets, and a set of anklets with tiny tinkling bells.

Fulani gold

Married Fulani women in northwest Africa wear enormous, circular earrings made from beaten gold. These earrings are a sign of a husband's wealth. As a man's wealth increases, more gold is beaten into his wife's earrings, making them even larger and heavier. Sometimes the earrings are so heavy that the woman has to have a string over her head to help support their weight.

On their wedding day, many Indian brides wear special jewellery and paint their faces with traditional patterns.

Early rulers and their wives

In early societies, marriage was often a way of gaining wealth and power. Marriages were mainly business arrangements rather than love affairs. Most portraits of early rulers and their wives are very formal. They simply show the couple seated side by side, splendidly dressed, and gazing straight ahead.

Ancient Greeks and Romans

By the time of the Ancient Greeks and Romans, poets, playwrights, and sculptors were celebrating the idea of love. Several Greek and Roman writers told the tragic story of Orpheus, who loved his wife Eurydice so deeply that he followed her into the **underworld** when she died. The Roman poet Horace composed haunting love poems to his perfect woman. Another Roman poet, Ovid, wrote a series of poems describing the romantic adventures of the gods and goddesses. These scenes of love between the gods were often shown in sculpture and carvings.

In everyday life, Greek and Roman marriages were often business-like arrangements. However, some writers and artists have provided evidence of close and loving marriages. The Roman writer Pliny wrote loving letters to his wife, telling her how much he missed her. A painting from the Roman town of Pompeii shows a young husband and wife, sitting shoulder-to-shoulder, gazing out together at the world.

In this 1st century CE portrait of a young Roman couple, the man holds a lawyer's scroll and the woman has a writing tablet. They are shown sitting very close together.

Medieval romance

In **medieval** Europe, poets, musicians, and artists created the ideal of courtly love. This involved a perfect knight promising undying love for a lady. According to the rules of **courtly love**, the knight was supposed to write poems and compose songs for the lady. He also had to perform great feats of bravery to show his love. However, the knight and his lady were never united.

During the **Middle Ages**, many songs and poems were written about love. Travelling musicians, known as **troubadours**, composed and sang songs about famous lovers.

Meanwhile, poets wrote "romances" telling stories of knights and their ladies. The most famous of these romances were the tales of King Arthur and his knights.

The romances were written out in manuscripts and illustrated with colourful pictures, known as **illuminations**. Some illuminations survive from the Middle Ages, showing famous lovers such as Sir Lancelot and Queen Guinevere.

This illumination comes from a 14th-century romance. It shows King Arthur and Queen Guinevere seated at a banquet, while Sir Lancelot kneels before his lady.

A wedding portrait?

'This painting used to be called *The Arnolfini Wedding* but is now called *The Arnolfini Portrait*. This is because in 1998 art experts became unsure whether a marriage ceremony is shown, or which members of the Arnolfini family this couple might be. Whoever they are, and whatever occasion the portrait shows, it is clear that the couple wanted to be pictured surrounded by their wealth. Some of the objects shown were very expensive in the 15th century; for example the woman's dress (she is not pregnant), the ornate mirror, and the huge candelabra.

The burning candle above the couple's heads may represent the constant flame of marriage. The small dog in the foreground is a symbol of faithfulness and love.

Marriage troubles

In his long poem *The Canterbury Tales*, the 14th-century poet Geoffrey Chaucer creates a character called "The Wife of Bath", who has been married five times. The Wife of Bath complains about the "woe" (sadness) that she has found in marriage. She talks about the tricks that she has played on her husbands and she is very humorous and down-to-earth about the trials of married life.

Jan van Eyck, *The Arnolfini Portrait* (1434). Experts are unsure that this is a marriage portrait, as originally thought. The artist has chosen to include a range of objects that may give clues to its meaning,

Renaissance images

In the 15th century, artists in Italy began to paint in a new way. They became very interested in the art of the Ancient Greeks and Romans. They admired the style of these **classical** artists, and tried to improve upon it. They also studied the world around them and tried to show people in a more realistic way. This movement in art was known as the **Renaissance**.

Many Renaissance artists copied the way that Greek and Roman artists showed scenes of love. They produced paintings and sculptures illustrating classical legends of love between the gods and goddesses.

Renaissance artists also painted portraits of married couples. In 1472, the powerful Duke Federico of Urbino paid the artist Piero Della Francesca to paint a portrait of himself and his wife. This famous double portrait shows the two splendid figures, both seen from the side, against a background of their kingdom. Duke Federico and his wife are richly dressed and both of them have a stern and commanding air. Piero's portrait shows two powerful people from wealthy families, who have made an excellent marriage to join their fortunes.

Later portraits

Portraits became fashionable in Europe during the 17th century, and many couples paid artists to paint them. These portraits of husbands and wives were usually very formal. They sometimes showed land, or items of wealth, which were part of the marriage agreement. Only a few artists managed to show more tender feelings. Around 1666, the Dutch artist Rembrandt van Rijn painted *The Jewish Bride*. This informal portrait shows the couple's close and loving relationship as the husband gently puts his hand over his wife's heart.

Rembrandt van Rijn, *The Jewish Bride* (c.1666). This portrait shows a friend of Rembrandt's with his young wife. In this **intimate** picture, the artist has managed to capture the tender feelings that the couple have for each other.

The game of love

During the 18th century, some artists in Europe presented a playful image of love. A group of French artists, led by Jean-Honoré Fragonard, painted light-hearted scenes of beautiful young women teasing their **suitors**. Fragonard's painting *The Swing* shows a young girl seated on a swing hanging from a tree. She kicks off a dainty shoe while a young man gazes up at her admiringly.

By the 1750s, some writers were starting to write about adventures in love. In 1749, Henry Fielding published *Tom Jones*. In this fast-moving story, a handsome young man meets a series of girls as he travels around the country. *Tom Jones* has been called the world's first comic novel. It presents a cheerful, light-hearted view of love, in which nobody gets seriously hurt.

Jean-Honoré Fragonard, *The Swing* (c. 1766). In this attractive picture, love is shown as a light-hearted game, rather than a serious emotion.

Not all 18th-century artists took such a cheerful view of relationships. The English artist William Hogarth produced a series of **engravings** showing what happens when people marry for money. The series was called *Marriage à la Mode*, which means "A fashionable marriage". It tells the story of a selfish couple, who make each other very unhappy and end in ruin. The story in the paintings may seem like a soap opera; however, the artist intended it to be a serious warning.

Romantic love

By the 19th century, writers and artists were starting to view love in a more romantic way. Lord Byron wrote a famous poem called *Don Juan*, about a hero who made every girl fall in love with him. Meanwhile, novelists such as Charlotte Brontë wrote emotional love stories. In her novel *Jane Eyre*, a poor woman falls in love with the rich and handsome Mr Rochester, who hides a terrible secret.

The English poet Tennyson was inspired by medieval stories of love. In his poem *The Idylls of the King*, Tennyson retells the great love story of Sir Lancelot and Queen Guinevere. Meanwhile, a group of English artists known as the **Pre-Raphaelites** were also inspired by knights and their ladies. These artists produced many fairytale images of romantic heroes and heroines in love.

Love in the opera

Many famous operas tell great love stories, but one of the most dramatic love stories of all is told in Georges Bizet's opera *Carmen*. The opera tells of a young man's doomed love for Carmen, a passionate gypsy girl. *Carmen* is full of magnificent **arias** on the theme of love. The story ends in tragedy when Carmen refuses to return the hero's love, so he stabs her in despair.

Bizet's opera *Carmen* is filled with dramatic scenes of love and passion. Here, Carmen, the gypsy girl, challenges her desperate lover.

Marc Chagall, *Birthday* (1915). This magical painting celebrates the happiness of married life. Chagall has included the tiny details of his life with Bella, such as her purse lying on the table.

Chagall's vision

In the 20th century, one artist stands out for his positive vision of love and marriage. The Russian-born painter Marc Chagall painted hundreds of images of his wife, Bella. He first met Bella when he was 22 years old, and instantly fell in love with her. From then on, most of Chagall's paintings featured Bella, sometimes on her own, but usually with him.

In many of his paintings, Chagall shows himself and Bella locked in each other's arms. Sometimes the couple are shown at home but often they are flying through the sky together. All Chagall's works have a **surreal**, dreamlike quality. His images of himself and Bella also give a powerful sense of happiness and contentment in their life together.

The Kiss

Two outstanding sculptors produced works called *The Kiss*. Auguste Rodin's sculpture was completed in 1886 and shows a couple in a passionate embrace. Rodin's figures are carefully observed and realistic, but the mood of the sculpture is strongly romantic. In contrast, Constantin Brancusi's two versions of *The Kiss* are much more abstract.

From 1908 to 1909, Brancusi worked on his first sculpture called *The Kiss*. Carved from a rectangular block of stone, it shows two block-like figures pressed together, face-to-face, with their arms held tightly around each other. In about 1945, Brancusi produced a second version of the same subject. In this work, the two embracing figures are very clearly carved from the same block of stone. It gives an even stronger impression that the two lovers belong to each other.

Lovers divided

Several artists in recent times have chosen to show the problems of relationships, rather than their joys. One powerful view of an unhappy marriage was painted by Walter Sickert in 1914. His painting is called *Ennui*, which is French for "boredom". It shows an unhappy couple in their living room, each turning away from the other. Both the husband and wife seem to be trapped in their marriage.

They both look longingly into the distance, as if they are dreaming of escape.

In 1928, the Belgian artist René Magritte painted a disturbing portrait called *The Lovers*. It shows a man and a woman posing for their portrait, but both of them have their heads covered in flowing white cloths. In this strange work, Magritte could be sending the message that it is impossible for two people to know each other properly or to make any real connection. Later the same year, Magritte produced a second painting, called *The Lovers II*. This shows the same figures kissing, with their heads still covered in white cloths.

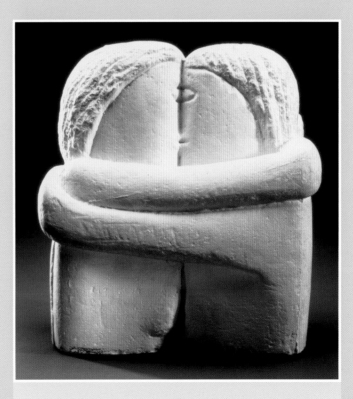

Constantin Brancusi, *The Kiss* (1908–1909). Brancusi carved two lovers from one stone block, to give a sense of closeness.

Happiness and contentment

Most artists agree that it is much harder to show happiness and contentment than it is to show sadness or pain. But some talented artists have managed to rise to the challenge. When you look at their works of art, you can feel the emotions of joy and pleasure.

Having fun

Some lively works of art show people having fun together. In the 16th century, the Flemish artist Pieter Bruegel painted scenes of ordinary people playing games, dancing, and feasting. In Bruegel's *Children's Games*, children are bowling hoops, playing tag, climbing over barrels, or twirling around in circles. Even the adults are joining in the fun.

Four hundred years after Bruegel, the French artist Henri Matisse created a series of images of women dancing together. These joyful pictures are painted in vivid reds, greens, and blues.

Pieter Bruegel, *The Wedding Dance* (c. 1566). Bruegel was a master at showing people having fun, although, if you look carefully, you will see that some are having more fun than others!

Frans Hals, *The Laughing Cavalier* (1624). Part of the appeal of this cheerful painting is that the subject is not laughing out loud. Instead, he seems to be just on the edge of bursting into a fit of laughter.

In his paintings of dancers, Matisse seems to be saying that this group of people is really enjoying being alive.

Sometimes a portrait can express joy and delight. The Dutch artist Frans Hals specialized in painting jolly, laughing people. His most famous painting, *The Laughing Cavalier* (1624), seems to invite the viewer to join in a joke that the artist and his subject are sharing.

Calm contentment

Some artists show a sense of calm contentment in the peaceful activities of daily life. The 17th-century Dutch artist Jan Vermeer often painted scenes from daily life. In his famous portrait of *The Milkmaid*, Vermeer shows a maid carefully pouring milk from a jug. Vermeer paints the scene in restful, pale colours and everything in his picture seems balanced and calm.

Statues of Maitreya, the Chinese god of good fortune, show a roly-poly character with an infectious laugh. Just the sight of Maitreya can make people feel better about their lives.

Many works of art from China, Japan, and southeast Asia show images of happiness. Often, these works are produced by **Buddhist** artists. There is also a long tradition in these parts of the world of showing a cheerful spirit of good fortune.

Images of the Buddha

The religion of Buddhism teaches people how to achieve a state of perfect happiness, known as **nirvana**. Statues of the Buddha often have a gently smiling expression, showing that he has achieved nirvana. Buddhists believe that by studying these images of the Buddha, they can be helped to gain a sense of peace and happiness.

Spirit of good fortune

Many Chinese sculptors and carvers produce images of a jolly laughing figure with a rounded belly. This figure is usually brightly painted and is often known by westerners as "the laughing Buddha". However, he does not represent the Buddha.

Hotei, the Japanese god of happiness, is shown pointing at the moon, asking the man in the moon how old he is.

The laughing figure's Chinese name is Maitreya. He was originally believed to be a spirit of good fortune, who carried presents in his bag to give to poor people and especially children. Carved figures of Maitreya are often found in Chinese shops and restaurants. The Chinese have an ancient tradition of rubbing Maitreya's belly. They hope that this action will bring them luck and good fortune.

Hotei

In Japan, artists show a laughing figure called Hotei. He was one of the seven lucky gods in traditional Japanese religion, and he was especially responsible for happiness. Hotei is often represented in miniature ivory carvings known as "netsuke". In traditional Japanese society, these carvings were often used as a toggle on a belt or a bag. This meant that people could keep an image of the god of happiness close to them at all times.

Climbing to happiness

The Buddhist temple of Borobodur on the Indonesian island of Java was built in the 8th century CE. It is shaped like a pyramid, with several levels. Each level of the temple is covered with religious carvings. Followers of the Buddhist religion are supposed to walk around each level of the temple, carefully studying all the images, until they reach the top. The process of climbing Borobodur is intended to help Buddhists achieve a state of happiness or nirvana.

Anger, violence, and hatred

The emotions of anger and violence can be powerful and dangerous. In many societies, these strong emotions are expressed in dances or ceremonies. In other ancient traditions, artists create images of gods or spirits that express angry feelings.

Fire ceremonies

Some groups of **Aboriginal people** in Australia hold dramatic fire dances. In these traditional ceremonies, dancers hold flaming branches and perform exaggerated movements. People hold fire dances when they have quarrelled or feel very angry. The dances help them to bring their angry feelings into the open. When they set fire to the branches and let them turn to ashes, they are solving the quarrel and letting go of their anger.

Angry gods

Some ancient societies have created images of angry or violent gods. One of the main Hindu gods is Vishnu, the preserver. For hundreds of years, he has been shown in Indian art as a fierce and violent god, who carries many weapons. However, Vishnu is usually shown as part of a **trio** of gods, which includes Rama, the creator, and Shiva, the destroyer. By representing all these aspects of life, **Hindu** artists aim to show that violence and destruction are only part of the larger cycle of life.

In Hindu art and mythology, gods often express emotions of anger and violence. This painting shows a fierce battle between the god Rama and Ravanna, king of the demons.

Artists and writers from Ancient Greece and Rome also portrayed angry gods. In particular, Roman statues of Jupiter often show the chief god in a rage, hurling thunderbolts down from heaven. Jupiter can be seen as an expression of the human emotion of anger. He is only one of many ancient gods, and each of them represents a different human emotion.

Fierce creatures

Native American art often features fierce and angry-looking creatures. The Mayan people, who lived in Central America from the 3rd century BCE to the 16th century CE, carved massive, snarling jaguar heads from stone. Meanwhile, Native Americans in the northwest decorated their **totem poles** with the heads of fierce grizzly bears. These aggressive creatures express the powerful emotions of rage and violence. In times of war, warriors danced around the totem pole to help them feel more violent and ready for battle. The fierce creatures also helped people to feel safe and protected.

Fearsome carvings, such as this bear, on totem poles express powerful feelings of aggression. They helped the Native Americans get into the mood for battle, and also helped to frighten off any enemies.

The spirit of Vajrapani

Buddhist art from Southeast Asia often features Vajrapani, the thunderbolt-bearer. He is usually shown dancing wildly inside a ring of flames, with a thunderbolt in his hand. Vajrapani appears to be a very violent figure, but in fact he represents the pure, human mind, when it has been freed from hatred. The ring of flames surrounding him shows that he has been transformed into a pure spirit. His thunderbolt shows his power to cut through the darkness of ignorance.

Violent warriors

For hundreds of years, painters and carvers have shown images of war. Many of these images seem to glory in the violence of battle. Carvings from Ancient Egypt, Greece, and Rome often show soldiers killing their enemies and even trampling their bodies underfoot. Paintings from the Mayan culture in Central America show fierce knights frightening their victims, while manuscripts from medieval Europe feature armed knights fighting bloody battles to the death.

In the 19th century, Japanese artists often showed **Samurai** warriors fighting each other. In these dramatic pictures, the warriors snarl at each other menacingly, as they wave their swords in the air.

The art of fighting

In many cultures, the practice of fighting was turned into a kind of art, with very strict moves and rules. The Ancient Greeks developed the sport of wrestling, which has continued until the present day. By the 15th century, young men in Europe were practising the art of fencing, a type of fighting with swords, which did not result in injury or death.

People in China began to practise **martial arts** as early as 5000 BCE. The Chinese created a range of fighting styles based on the movements of different creatures, such as the crane, the tiger, and the praying mantis.

Martial arts became established in Japan around the 12th century CE. The Japanese developed many different styles of martial arts including judo, aikido, and karate. During the 20th century, interest in Chinese and Japanese martial arts spread to the West.

In all the martial arts, the aim is to change the violent act of fighting into something disciplined and calm. Martial arts can be seen as a kind of body art, rather like a ballet.

A 19th-century Japanese print, showing a Samurai warrior in action.

Going berserk

According to Viking legend, Odin, the god of war, charged into battle surrounded by savage warriors known as "berserkers". Berserkers were incredibly strong and fought like mad bears. Before a battle, berserkers worked themselves up into a frenzy by biting on their shields. Some ancient images of berserkers survive, showing this frightening custom. The phrase "going berserk" comes from the name of these mythical warriors.

These two Viking knights are part of an ivory chess set. The figure on the right is a berserker. He is working himself into a frenzy by biting hard on his shield.

Expressing rage

Art has always been a useful weapon for attacking society. Through their art, artists can show their rage about the things that are happening around them. Art can also help to raise public anger and awareness, and even lead to change.

Hogarth and Daumier

In the 17th century, the artist Jan Steen painted *The Effects of Intemperance*. It shows a drunken mother slumped on a step, and a small boy stealing money from her pocket. With this picture, Jan Steen was commenting on the behaviour he saw in his society, and saying that parents should set better examples for their children. Do you think similar issues concern people today?

A century later, Honoré Daumier attacked French society through his brilliant cartoons. He concentrated on the terrible life of the poor in the city of Paris. One of Daumier's most famous cartoons shows a poor man gazing though the window of a restaurant at the rich people feasting inside. Daumier also attacked the French government in his art. Some of his cartoons show government tax collectors as inhuman, rat-like creatures.

Protest in Germany

In the 1930s, many rich people in Germany enjoyed an extremely extravagant lifestyle and ignored the problems of the poor. A group of German artists used their art to protest against this selfish way of life. Max Beckmann, George Grosz, and Otto Dix produced shocking images of life in Berlin. They showed the rich people enjoying the bars and cafes as very ugly, with cruel and stupid expressions. The artists used vivid colours and a bold, violent painting style to make their protest.

Diego Rivera

For hundreds of years, the Mexican people were cruelly treated by the Spanish conquerors of their land, until they finally rose in rebellion in 1810, and won their independence in 1821. One famous Mexican artist made an angry visual protest against this treatment of his people by the Spanish. In the early 20th century, Diego Rivera created a series of gigantic **murals** on the theme of the Mexican people's struggle for freedom. Even though Rivera was showing events that happened in the past, his very public works of art still expressed the Mexican people's spirit of anger and resistance.

The Punk movement

"Punk" art, music, and fashion emerged in Britain in the 1970s. Punk music was loud, raucous, and angry, and Punk art and fashion were deliberately shocking. The Punk movement expressed the rage of young people at their powerlessness in modern society.

A scene from a mural by Diego Rivera, *Epic of the Mexican People* (1929-1935). Rivera's mural expresses the artist's anger at the terrible sufferings of his people. In this scene, he shows the Spanish conquerors of Mexico treating the Mexican people as slaves.

Grief, loss, and mourning

All societies have special rituals and ceremonies to mark a person's death. These ancient customs help people to grieve for those who have died. In some societies, there are many art forms connected with mourning and burying the dead.

African funeral dances

Many people in Africa still perform traditional dances and ceremonies for the dead. In these dances, people wear specially carved and painted funeral masks, representing the spirits who will guide the souls of the dead people. Each tribe has its own designs for funeral masks.

The Dogon people of West Africa carve wooden funeral masks to look like animal heads. Many of these masks also have a tall wooden structure rising from the top of the wearer's head. Dogon dancers wear these masks to perform a striking funeral dance. The dancers take huge leaps into the air and then plunge down low, so that the tips of their masks sweep the ground.

Aboriginal grave posts

The Tiwi Aboriginal people live on Melville and Bathurst Islands, off the northern coast of Australia. They perform a ceremony which is intended to guide the souls of the dead to the spirit world.

A set of carved grave posts, made by the Tiwi people, who live on islands near Australia. The grave posts represent the spirits of the dead. People express their grief for the dead by performing mourning ceremonies around these posts.

During their ceremony, the Tiwi people dance around a set of tall carved and painted poles, known as grave posts. These posts represent the dead members of their **clan**. The posts are carved to look like a human body and their decorations are similar in style to Tiwi body paintings. Towards the end of the ceremony, special bark baskets are broken over the grave posts. This is meant to show that the spirits of the dead have been set free.

The Day of the Dead

In present-day Mexico, people still celebrate the Day of the Dead. According to tradition, this is a day when people can communicate with dead members of their family. Mexican artists and craft workers create a range of images that are all supposed to make fun of death. They include puppets in the form of skeletons, and also model figures of skeletons performing a range of actions. Models even show wedding couples, footballers, and policemen.

These skeleton puppets are part of a procession to celebrate the Day of the Dead. By creating humorous figures of the dead, Mexican artists make fun of death.

Preparing for the after life

In many ancient cultures, people believed that they went to live in another world when they died. They also believed that dead people could take their possessions with them. Rulers were buried with incredible treasures, ready for their life in the next world.

Egyptian mummies

The Ancient Egyptians buried their **pharaohs** in massive pyramids. Inside the pyramids were paintings that showed the pharaoh's life on earth. The Egyptians also tried to preserve the pharaoh's body by **embalming** it in special ointments, and wrapping it in linen strips, to form a **mummy**. The mummified bodies of the pharaohs were placed inside elaborate coffins, made from wood and precious metals.

The most famous surviving Egyptian coffin case belongs to the boy pharaoh, Tutankhamun. His coffin is made from solid gold. It shows the young ruler staring straight ahead, holding his emblems of office, and dressed in his full, ceremonial robes.

Mississippi monuments

Around 700 CE, Native American farmers in the Mississippi valley began to bury their chiefs with pots, carvings, and ornaments under large, flat-topped mounds in their town centres. On the top of the mounds, priests carried out ceremonies in honour of the dead chiefs. The biggest of these early towns, Cahokia, had over a hundred burial mounds.

Pueblo burial pots

The Native American Pueblo people lived in the southwest of North America. They buried their chiefs with special burial pots. Pueblo burial pots were painted with designs that showed gods and spirits. They also had a hole pierced in their base. The hole allowed the spirits to be released. This meant that the spirits were able to guide the dead chiefs to the next world.

Tomb sculpture

In medieval Europe, skilled carvers and sculptors created statues of the dead. These lifelike statues were known as **effigies**. Effigies of dead knights or kings were carved from stone, wood, or **alabaster**. These figures lie on top of their tomb, often hand-in-hand with their wife. Around the sides of the tomb, carvers often showed portraits of the dead person's family, kneeling or standing in a row.

The tradition of carving effigies of the dead continued until the 19th century. By this time, a new tradition had developed. People created fancy gravestones decorated with carving and sculpture. Graveyards dating from the 19th century are filled with weeping **cherubs** and angels carved from marble and stone.

A 13th-century marble effigy from the tomb of the French King, Philippe III. Medieval sculptors created realistic images of the dead. This was a way of showing respect to a person who had died. Effigies also helped to remind people of the dead.

Remembering the dead

In the 19th century, many artists became very interested in showing emotions. They produced some powerful expressions of mourning and grief.

Arthur Hughes' *Home from the Sea* tells a sad story of two children whose parents have recently died. It shows a young boy and his older sister in an English country graveyard. The boy is dressed in a sailor suit and has clearly just returned from a long sea journey. He has thrown himself face-down in despair on the grass, while his sister, dressed in black, looks on sadly. By simply showing the young boy's back, Hughes has cleverly placed the viewer of the picture in the awkward position of a concerned but helpless onlooker. When you look at this picture, you want to comfort the boy, but you know you can't.

The French artist Gustave Courbet was working around the same time as Arthur Hughes, but in a less **sentimental** style. His painting *The Burial at Ornans* shows a country funeral. The mood of Courbet's picture is solemn and quiet. There are no dramatic displays of emotion. Nevertheless, the grief of the old women is dignified and convincing.

Arthur Hughes, *Home from the Sea* (1863). Hughes' painting tells a tragic story. The hopeful spring flowers in the graveyard contrast strongly with the sadness of the boy.

Despair and lamentation

The German artist Käthe Kollwitz lived through two World Wars and lost a son and a grandson in the conflicts. In her drawings and prints, she concentrates on the desperate emotions of women as they mourn their dead husbands and sons. These haunting images include figures stretching out their hands in agony, or crumpled up in despair.

Käthe Kollwitz also produced some very powerful sculptures. One huge work shows a kneeling man and a woman, each lost in their own sadness. The woman is bowed over in grief, while the man wraps his arms around his body as he stares sightlessly ahead.

Another sculpture, called *Lamentation*, shows a woman's grief-stricken face almost entirely covered by her hands.

Saying goodbye

Usually, the emotions of grief and loss are associated with mourning and death. But one early 20th-century painting provides a different image of sadness. In the 1850s, the English artist Ford Madox Brown painted *Last of England*. This painting shows a young man and woman on a crowded ship, setting off to start a new life in America. In the distance are the cliffs of Dover, but the couple simply stare ahead. Their faces show sadness, because they are leaving their home, but also determination to face the future bravely.

Ford Madox Brown, *Last of England* (1855). The faces of the young couple staring out to sea register a mixture of emotions – sadness, anxiety, and determination. Each of them is lost in their own thoughts, but they also clasp hands, gaining silent support from each other.

Sickness and pain

Some artists have drawn on their own experience of sickness to produce disturbing images of suffering. By studying these works of art, it is possible to gain some idea of what it is like to suffer pain and illness.

Goya and his doctor

When he was 73 years old, the great Spanish artist Francisco de Goya suffered a serious illness and nearly died. In the following year, Goya painted a portrait of himself with his doctor. The painting is called *Self-Portrait with Doctor Arrieta* and it is dedicated to Goya's doctor.

In Goya's frightening painting, the sick artist stares into the distance while his feeble hands fumble with his bedclothes. In contrast, his doctor is strong and determined. The doctor holds his patient firmly as he forces him to take his medicine, and his face glows healthily in contrast to the artist's pale and puffy one. Meanwhile, several shadowy characters hover around the patient's bed. These ghostly figures may be real visitors, or they may be nightmare creatures produced by Goya's feverish imagination. The painting leaves a terrifying impression of the helpless artist close to death.

Munch's sister

The Scandinavian artist Edvard Munch was haunted by memories of sickness and death. His mother and sister died from **tuberculosis** while he was still a child and Munch himself suffered from serious illnesses. This was a subject he returned to many times in his art.

In the years 1885 to 1886, Munch painted *The Sick Child.* In this simple but powerful painting, a pale young girl sits up in bed. She turns towards her mother, who bows her head in distress. Although she is clearly ill and weak, the girl smiles gently at her mother, in an attempt to comfort her. The painting contains few details of the room. Instead, Munch concentrates on the relationship between the sick girl and her mother.

Frida Kahlo

The Mexican artist Frida Kahlo was in constant pain. She was seriously injured in a car accident when she was 18 years old, and had to spend long stretches of time in bed, or in hospital having operations. Kahlo's art reflects her suffering. In *The Little Deer* (1946) she paints herself with the body of a wounded stag pierced by arrows. *The Broken Column* (painted in 1944) shows Frida with a fractured spine, wearing a body brace, and punctured by nails.

Frida Kahlo, *The Mask of Madness* (1945). At times during her life, Frida Kahlo felt she was on the verge on madness. Here, she shows herself putting on the mask of a mad woman. However, the mask doesn't stop her suffering. There are tears falling from its eyes.

Fear, loneliness, and isolation

Many artists have produced images of fear, both in paintings and in sculpture. Often, these works show people reacting to a frightening situation, such as the fires of hell or a storm at sea. A few works portray a single figure gripped by terror.

Images of terror

In 1907, the French sculptor André Derain carved *Crouching Man* from a single block of stone. Derain's sculpture shows a man with his knees raised, protecting his head with his hands. Just looking at this simple figure can be enough to fill you with fear. The fear is made more powerful because you are left to imagine exactly what the crouching man is hiding from.

Edvard Munch's painting *The Scream* also has a powerful impression on the viewer (see page 5). Here, the screaming figure seems to be making a desperate appeal for help. It seems as if he is begging you to rescue him from some unseen horror.

André Derain, *Crouching Man* (1907). This simple sculpture is a powerful expression of fear. The crouching man could be any age or race, but his feelings are unmistakable.

Edward Hopper, *People in the Sun* (1960). People relaxing in the sun might seem a cheerful subject. But Hopper's characters seem isolated, and the landscape seems empty.

Suspense and horror

During the 19th century, writers in Europe and America began to write stories, novels, and poems that were specially designed to frighten their readers. These works of mystery and suspense were known as **gothic horror** stories.

One of the early masters of gothic horror was the American author Edgar Allan Poe. His famous story, *The Fall of the House of Usher*, written in 1839, tells a scary tale of disease and madness, set in a crumbling, haunted mansion.

In the 1930s, film producers in Hollywood began to create horror movies. Alfred Hitchcock wrote and directed the famous films *Psycho* and *The Birds*. Hitchcock was brilliant at building up suspense. Later, many other film directors copied his techniques. Horror films are still very popular today.

Loneliness and isolation

By the 20th century, some artists were expressing a powerful sense of loneliness and isolation. They recognized the fact that people in modern society could feel very alone, even when they were surrounded by others.

One artist stands out for his portraits of loneliness. Edward Hopper lived from 1882 to 1967, and painted scenes of American life. Hopper's paintings show lonely, drifting characters in city streets, trains, and all-night diners. Hopper also painted people in the countryside, or by the sea. These lonely characters are often shown sitting in deckchairs, facing the sun. They are each locked in their own private world and none of them turns to talk to another.

Depression and despair

Like other people, artists can suffer from **depression**. As creative, sensitive people, artists sometimes use art as a way to work through their feelings. Sometimes it is hard to judge what they were trying to express, because we have our own feelings about every work of art that we look at.

A tortured genius

In 1888, van Gogh invited his artist friend Paul Gauguin to stay with him. The two of them painted in his studio and got on very well at first, but later they quarrelled bitterly. The argument led to van Gogh cutting his ear lobe and having to have it bandaged up. Soon after this van Gogh went to a **psychiatric hospital**. While he was there he experienced a deep depression. He never saw Gauguin again.

During the period that van Gogh was depressed, he painted several self-portraits and landscapes. In his self-portrait with the bandaged ear, the artist stares out from the canvas. His yellow skin makes him look ill; however, we know from letters that he wrote to his brother that van Gogh associated the colour yellow with hope. This example shows how difficult is it to interpret a person's feeling from their artwork. Only van Gogh himself could really explain what he was feeling at the time.

Vincent van Gogh, *Self-Portrait with a Bandaged Ear and Pipe* (1889). Despite the brightness of the painting's colours, the artist seems drained of life and hope.

Putting on a mask

Several artists have explored the idea of putting on a mask in order to hide their true feelings from the world. In the 19th century, the Belgian artist James Ensor produced some very disturbing pictures of groups of people, all wearing masks. Some wear grinning skull masks, some are clowns and pirates, and some are highly painted ladies. Ensor's masked figures seem frightening and unreal.

When you look at these paintings, you wonder: "Who are the real people underneath the masks?"

Perhaps Ensor's most alarming image of all is his *Self-Portrait Surrounded by Masks*. Here, Ensor shows himself wearing a feathered hat in the centre of a picture that is entirely made up of hideous masked faces. This painting raises the difficult question: "Which is the artist's true self?"

Acting the clown

In the 20th century, the great Spanish artist Pablo Picasso produced many paintings of **harlequins** – a kind of clown in a colourful costume. Picasso was fascinated by the idea of putting on a costume and becoming a different sort of being.

In France, Edgar Degas and Henri de Toulouse-Lautrec painted female clowns relaxing off-stage. Meanwhile, Georges Rouault produced striking images of mournful clowns wearing heavy make-up. All these works show the contrast between the real people and the cheerful smiling masks that they show to the public.

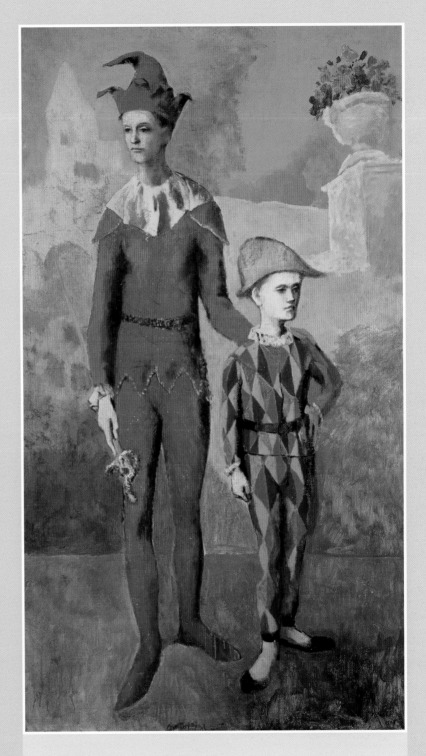

Pablo Picasso, *Acrobat and Young Harlequin* (1905). The solemn faces of the clowns contrast with their playful costumes. Why do you think Picasso chose to paint them?

Dreams, nightmares, and fantasies

From the time of the earliest civilizations, people have recognized that dreams, nightmares, and **fantasies** can be a rich source of inspiration for artists. Artists, musicians, and writers often use images that come to them in sleep. They also use their imagination to create fantasy figures and scenes.

Dreams and nightmares

In the 18th century, artists became very interested in exploring the world of dreams and the imagination. The Italian artist Giovanni Piranesi showed towering dreamlike buildings that could not possibly exist in the real world.

Sometimes these buildings are decorated with grinning faces and sometimes they are filled with terrifying machinery. Piranesi has been described as the father of fantasy art.

Henry Fuseli was a Swiss-born painter who explored the world of dreams and nightmares. His most famous work is *The Nightmare*, which was painted in 1781. This frightening picture shows a young woman stretched over a bed with a look of terror on her sleeping face. Standing over her bed is a staring winged horse, and a grinning demon sits at her bedside.

Henri Fuseli, *The Nightmare* (1781). Fuseli's haunting painting gives a real sense of how it feels to have a nightmare. His monstrous figures, hovering over the helpless woman on the bed, are terrifying but ghostly, as if they are not really there.

Another artist who depicted a nightmare world was the English painter Richard Dadd, who lived from 1817 to 1886. Dadd suffered from mental illness and spent the last twenty years of his life in a psychiatric hospital. His paintings are filled with tiny goblins, dwarves, and fairies. Dadd worked on one painting, *The Fairy Feller*, for nine years, adding more and more fantastic figures and details.

Gentle daydreams

In the 19th century, a group of English artists known as the Pre-Raphaelites aimed to create a sense of dreamlike mystery in their work. Several of their paintings show romantic figures, gazing dreamily into the distance. The most famous of these images is Dante Gabriel Rossetti's *The Day Dream*. The painting shows a beautiful young girl surrounded by creepers of honeysuckle. On her lap is the book that has inspired her dreams. She seems like a princess inside a fairytale forest.

Dante Gabriel Rossetti, *The Day Dream* (1880). A girl is surrounded by honeysuckle. According to legend, the scent of honeysuckle can make girls fall in love.

Painting the Dreamtime

The Aboriginal people of Australia have a traditional belief that their world was created many thousands of years ago in a time known as the Dreamtime. According to Aboriginal beliefs, powerful Spirit Ancestors wandered over the world during the Dreamtime, creating the Earth and everything on it. Many Aboriginal paintings show events from the Dreamtime, when the Spirit Ancestors created rocks, plants, animals, and people.

Exploring the subconscious

By the start of the 20th century, people recognized that dreams, nightmares, and fantasies were all produced by the **subconscious mind**. Many artists became very interested in the idea of the subconscious. One group in particular, known as the **Surrealists**, tried to show the surprising images produced by the subconscious mind.

Automatic art

Some Surrealist artists aimed to create works of art using only their subconscious mind. They closed their eyes and let their hands draw freely. These experimental works were known as "automatic art". Many artists use automatic drawing as the starting point for a work of art. The paintings of the Spanish artist, Joan Miró, were often based on automatic drawing.

Surreal dreams

Some Surrealist artists created images based on the surprising world of dreams. In particular, Salvador Dalî created amazing dreamlike landscapes. In Dalî's paintings, objects do not obey the same rules as they do in normal, "waking" life.

Another Surrealist artist, Giorgio de Chirico, painted strange landscapes filled with ruined columns and life-like statues. De Chirico's landscapes are very brightly lit, and the objects in his scenes have long, inky shadows.

The Belgian René Magritte also explored the surreal world of dreams. His paintings contain unexplained images such as flying umbrellas and giant apples. Magritte's works are often very disturbing, as they make the viewer question the rules of our everyday world.

Chagall's dreams

The Russian artist Marc Chagall was not a member of the Surrealist movement, but his paintings have a strongly dream-like quality. Chagall created an imaginary world in which he could fly. In his paintings, objects and people from different parts of his life are all brought together in a way that often happens in dreams (see page 22).

Fantasy art

Over the last twenty years, "fantasy art" has become very popular. Fantasy art is influenced by fairy tales and by science fiction and is often reproduced on posters. Fantasy artists paint in a detailed, realistic style, using vivid, almost **fluorescent** colours. Some artists show fairytale images such as castles, wizards, and dragons, while others create images of planets, often inspired by science fiction.

In Giorgio de Chirico's surreal painting *Song of the South*, the spirit of the guitar music seems to fill the musician's whole body.

Art without emotion?

By the mid 20th century, many painters and sculptors were producing abstract art. The focus was on form, shapes, line, colour, and energy. These abstract works of art tend to have no obvious subject. It can be difficult to make out figures and objects, although they might be there. The viewer needs to spend time thinking about what the work might mean to them personally.

Painting with feeling

In the 1950s, a number of artists produced abstract works that were intended to express their feelings. In particular, a group called the **Abstract Expressionists** painted works that were filled with emotional energy. The Abstract Expressionists were mainly based in the United States. They included Jackson Pollock and Mark Rothko.

Jackson Pollock covered vast canvases with trails and splashes of paint, creating bold and dramatic compositions. Many people see Pollock's works as powerful expressions of energy, excitement, and even violence.

Mark Rothko created compositions from large areas of colour that blend subtly into each other. Many of his paintings were made up of just two colours forming two horizontal blocks. Looking at a Rothko painting can produce feelings of peacefulness in a viewer, similar to the effect of looking at a landscape.

No emotions?

A group of abstract artists called the **Minimalists** went even further. Artists such as Carl Andre and Sol LeWitt believed that the beauty of simple lines, pure shapes, or colour could only be appreciated when seen on their own. Does this simple approach mean their art has no emotion? Or do people feel a connection with the harmony and balance of the simple shapes?

Reacting to art

Some people find it difficult to open their mind to the ideas in art. It is always important to remember that everyone's response to an artwork is valid, even though the art may mean something completely different to each person.

A new kind of emotion?

In the early 20th century, the Russian artist Kasimir Malevich produced a series of abstract paintings called *White on White* that were painted entirely in white. Malevich believed that by looking at his paintings, viewers could rise above their ordinary emotions, and reach a new kind of feeling. Malevich called his style of art "Suprematism" because he thought it expressed "supreme" emotions.

Jackson Pollock, *Free Form* (1946). Even though Pollock's paintings have no obvious subject, they still express powerful emotions. Pollock used colour as a way to express his emotions. Why do you think he chose red and black for this painting?

Map and Further reading

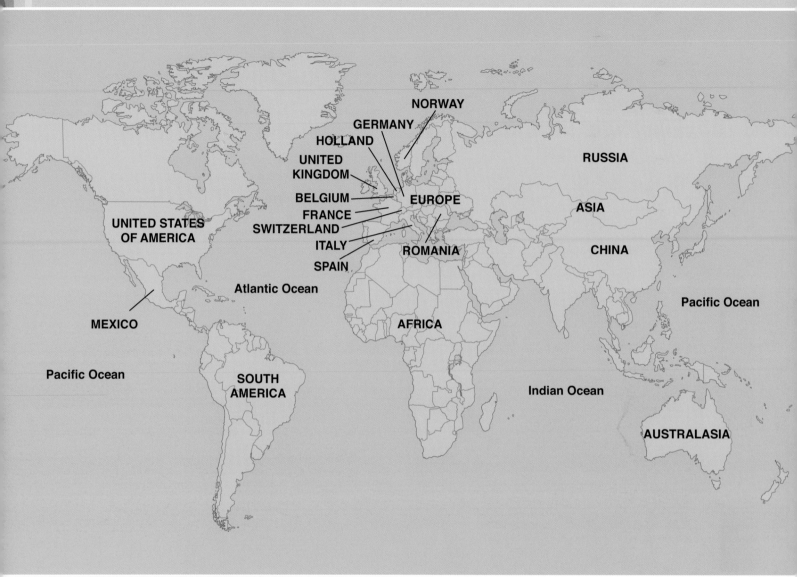

NORWAY
GERMANY
HOLLAND
UNITED KINGDOM
BELGIUM
FRANCE
SWITZERLAND
ITALY
SPAIN
EUROPE
ROMANIA
RUSSIA
ASIA
CHINA
UNITED STATES OF AMERICA
MEXICO
Atlantic Ocean
Pacific Ocean
SOUTH AMERICA
AFRICA
Indian Ocean
Pacific Ocean
AUSTRALASIA

Map of the world

This map shows you roughly where in the world some key works of art mentioned in this book were produced. The countries marked on the map relate to entries in the timeline, opposite.

Further reading

History in Art series
(Raintree, 2005)

Directions in Art series
(Heinemann Library, 2003)

Art in History series
(Heinemann Library, 2001)

Eyewitness Art: Looking at Paintings, Jude Welton, (Dorling Kindersley, 1994)

Timeline

This timeline provides approximate dates for some key works of art. The entries are linked to countries marked on the map of the world, opposite.

c.100s   Mayan artists start to show snarling jaguar heads and violent warriors (modern-day Mexico)

c.1000s The tradition of "courtly love" is established in medieval Europe

1300s   Chinese artists begin the tradition of painting formal ancestor portraits

1434   Jan van Eyck paints *The Arnolfini Portrait* (modern-day Belgium)

c.1600s Sculptors in West Africa portray proud rulers and queen mothers

1624   Frans Hals paints *The Laughing Cavalier* (Holland)

1666   Rembrandt van Rijn paints *The Jewish Bride* (Holland)

c.1767   Jean-Honoré Fragonard paints *The Swing* (France)

1777   John Singleton Copley paints *The Copley Family* (USA)

1781   Henri Fuseli paints *The Nightmare* (Switzerland)

1820   Francisco de Goya paints *Self-Portrait with Doctor Arrieta* (Spain)

1860   Ford Madox Brown paints *Last of England* (UK)

1863   Arthur Hughes completes *Home from the Sea* (UK)

1870s   Mary Cassatt and Berthe Morisot start to produce their portraits of mothers and children (USA, France)

1871   James McNeill Whistler paints *Arrangement in Grey and Black: Portrait of the Painter's Mother* (USA)

1880   Dante Gabriel Rossetti paints *The Day Dream* (UK)

1886   Auguste Rodin completes his sculpture, *The Kiss* (France)

1889   Vincent van Gogh paints *Self-Portrait with a Bandaged Ear* (Holland)

1893   Edvard Munch paints *The Scream* (Norway)

1900s   Käthe Kollwitz starts to produce her powerful works expressing grief and loss (Germany)

         Pablo Picasso starts to paint images of harlequins (Spain)

1907   André Derain creates *Crouching Man* (France)

c.1910   Marc Chagall starts to produce his dreamlike paintings, expressing his love of his wife Bella (Russia)

1912   Constantin Brancusi sculpts his second version of *The Kiss* (Romania)

1913   Kasimir Malevich founds Suprematism (Russia)

1914   Walter Sickert paints *Ennui* (UK)

1928   René Magritte paints two versions of *The Lovers* (Belgium)

1930s   Max Beckmann, George Grosz, and Otto Dix produce angry paintings attacking German society

1944   Frida Kahlo paints *The Broken Column* (Mexico)

1950s   Jackson Pollock leads the Abstract Expressionist movement (USA)

1960   Alfred Hitchcock directs the horror film *Psycho* (USA/ UK)

         Edward Hopper paints *People in the Sun* (USA)

1970s   The Punk movement emerges in Britain

Glossary

Aboriginal people people who have lived in a country for thousands of years, before later settlers arrived

abstract showing an idea rather than a thing

Abstract Expressionists a group of artists working in New York in the 1940s. The Abstract Expressionists used an abstract style to show emotions.

alabaster white stone that looks like marble

ancestors family members who lived a long time ago

archaeologist someone who studies the past by uncovering old objects or buildings and examining them carefully

aria a song for a single performer in an opera

Buddhist someone who follows the religion of Buddhism. Buddhists believe that you should not become too attached to material things. They also believe that you live many lives in different bodies.

cherub a young angel

clan a group of people who share the same ancestors and customs

classical in the style of the Ancient Greeks and Romans

courtly love a set of manners for young men in love that was developed in the Middle Ages

courtship the act of paying special attention to a person who you wish to marry

depression a strong feeling of sadness and despair

effigy a statue of a dead person carved on their tomb

embalm to preserve a dead body with special liquids and ointments

engraving a picture printed from an ink-covered plate that has been carved by an artist using a knife. Engravings can be made from wood or steel plates.

estate a large area of land belonging to a family

fantasy something that someone imagines, which could not happen in real life

fluorescent very bright

formal stiff, well-behaved, and not casual

fresco wall painting done on wet plaster

gothic horror a style of writing that concentrates on scary characters and scenes

harlequin a type of clown who wears a colourful costume with diamond patterns

Hindu a follower of Hinduism, the main religion and culture of India and Nepal

illumination a small painted picture in a medieval hand-written book

Impressionist a style of painting in which artists try to show the impression that something has on their senses

informal relaxed and casual

intimate very close and personal

martial arts styles of fighting and self defence that come from the Far East

media a method used by an artist. Drawing, painting, and sculpture are all different media.

medieval belonging to the period from approximately 1000 CE to 1450 CE

Middle Ages the period of history between approximately 1000 CE and 1450 CE

Minimalists a group of artists and musicians who try to make their work as simple as possible. Minimalist artists use simple shapes and a limited range of flat colours.

mummy a dead body that has been preserved in special liquids and wrapped in cloth so that it will last for a very long time

mural wall painting

nirvana a state of perfect understanding and contentment that Buddhists aim to reach

pharaoh an Egyptian ruler

porcelain fine china

portray to show something or someone through art, music or writing

Pre-Raphaelites a group of 19th-century artists who tried to return to the style and subjects of the Middle Ages

psychiatric hospital a hospital for people with mental health problems

Renaissance a movement in art and learning that took place in Europe between the 14th and 16th centuries. Renaissance artists aimed to produce more realistic works of art than before, and were partly inspired by the art of the Ancient Greeks and Romans.

rituals a set of actions that are always performed in the same way

samurai a Japanese warrior

sari a long piece of light material, worn draped around the body. Saris are worn mainly by Indian women and girls.

sculptor someone who makes works of art from stone, wood, metal or other materials

semi-abstract work that concentrates on ideas rather than things, but whose subject can still be recognized

sentimental very emotional

subconscious mind the part of the mind that works without people being aware of it. Dreams come from the subconscious mind.

suitor someone who tries to persuade another person to marry them

surreal dream-like, and not like the real world

Surrealists a group of artists who show dreamlike images. The Surrealist Movement began in France in the 1920s.

totem pole a carved and painted pole made by Native Americans. Totem poles have special religious meanings.

trio a group of three people or things

troubadours medieval musicians who travelled from castle to castle, entertaining people with their love songs

tuberculosis a serious lung disease

underworld an area under the earth where people went to live after they had died, according to Ancient Greek and Roman beliefs

Index

Aboriginal peoples 28, 34–35, 47
abstract art 14, 23, 50
Abstract Expressionists 50
African peoples 6, 11, 14, 15, 34
Andre, Carl 50
anger and violence 28–33
automatic art 48

beadwork 14
Beckmann, Max 32
berserkers 31
Bizet, Georges 21
body painting 14
Brancusi, Constantin 23
Brown, Ford Madox 39
Bruegel, Pieter 24
Buddhist art 26, 27, 29
burial mounds 36
burial pots 36

Cassatt, Mary 10
Chagall, Marc 22, 48
Copley, John Singleton 8
Courbet, Gustave 38

Dadd, Richard 47
Dalî, Salvador 48
dances 14, 28, 34
Daumier, Honoré 32
de Chirico, Giorgio 48, 49
de Hooch, Pieter 10
death 34–39
Degas, Edgar 45
depression and despair 44
Derain, André 42
Dix, Otto 32
dreams and nightmares 22, 46–49

Easter Island 7
Egypt, Ancient 30, 36
engravings 21
Ensor, James 44-45
Escher, M.C. 12
family portraits 6–13
fantasy art 48
fear 42-43
Fielding, Henry 20
films 43

Fragonard, Jean-Honoré 20
frescoes 8
Fuseli, Henry 46

Gainsborough, Thomas 8, 9
Gauguin, Paul 44
gothic horror 43
Goya, Francisco de 40
graves 34–36
Greece, Ancient 16, 30
grief and mourning 34–39
Grosz, George 32

Hals, Frans 25
happiness 24–27
Hitchcock, Alfred 43
Hogarth, William 21, 32
Hopper, Edward 43
Horace 16
Hughes, Arthur 38

illuminations 17
Impressionists 10

jewellery 14, 15
John, Augustus 12

Kahlo, Frida 40, 41
Kollwitz, Käthe 39

LeWitt, Sol 50
loneliness and isolation 43
love and marriage 14–23

Magritte, René 23, 48
Malevich, Kasimir 50
Mantegna, Andrea 8
martial arts 30
masks 34, 44–45
Matisse, Henri 24–25
Maya 29, 30
Middle Ages 17, 30, 36
Minimalists 50
Miro, Joan 48
Moore, Henry 11
Morisot, Berthe 10
mummies 36
Munch, Edvard 4, 5, 40, 42

murals 32

Native Americans 29, 36
novels and short stories 20, 21, 43

operas 21
Ovid 16

Picasso, Pablo 45
Piero della Francesca 19
Piranesi, Giovanni 46
Pliny 16
poetry 16, 17, 18, 19, 21
Pollock, Jackson 50, 51
pottery 36
Pre-Raphaelites 21, 47
Punk movement 32

Rembrandt van Rijn 19
Renaissance 19
Reynolds, Sir Joshua 8
Rivera, Diego 32, 33
Rodin, Auguste 23
Rome, Ancient 16, 29, 30
Rossetti, Dante Gabriel 47
Rothko, Mark 50
Rouault, Georges 45
Rubens, Peter Paul 12

Samurai warriors 30
sculpture 6–7, 11, 23, 29, 34, 35, 36, 39, 42
Shakespeare, William 19
Sickert, Walter 23
sickness and pain 40-41
subconscious mind 48
Surrealism 22, 48

totem poles 29
Toulouse-Lautrec, Henri de 45

Van Eyck, Jan 18
Van Gogh, Vincent 12, 44
Vermeer, Jan 25
Vikings 31

Whistler, James McNeill 12-13